So You Want to Go Contracting?

A Step-by-Step Guide to the World of Freelancing, Interim Management and Contracting

Paul Taylor

So You Want to Go Contracting

CreateSpace Independent Publishing Platform
Copyright © 2018, Paul Taylor

Published in the United States of America

180501-01079-2

ISBN-13: 978-1729506844
ISBN-10: 1729506844

Contents

Acknowledgements

I would like to dedicate this book to my wife and two daughters because without their support, I would not have been able to achieve anything.

Introduction

Differences between Freelance, Interim and Contract Work

Before I get into detail, I would like to explore what is the difference between freelance, interim management and contract work.

These different phrases are used interchangeably. There is a large amount of debate on this topic. Although there is no agreed definition of these terms.

However, typically, a freelancer will work with separate clients across several different sites. They will charge their clients an hourly rate or a fixed price. They will work on their own premises and engage in a creative industry such as photography, accountancy, or architecture.

Whereas a contractor will work on a single client site for a fixed period of time (such as several months) with a fixed hourly or daily rate. These projects tend to be based on technology and / or change management.

Finally an interim manager is often brought into to perform a management role as a 'stop gap', while the client looks to recruit a permanent replacement.

However, I have worked with many freelancers who have worked only with one client and many contractors who have several clients.

From my experience, the job roles of freelancer, interim manager and contractor make no real difference. They are interchangeable. As a freelancer, interim manager or contractor, you will either be hired (or not) by a client because of your skills and experience.

Therefore, the same approach, hints, and tips outlined in this book can be followed by all three.

However for the purposes of this book, I will assume that these terms are the same and I will use the term "contractor" to cover all three. If there are specific differences then these will be highlighted.

My Background

I have been contracting now for nearly 11 years and I have enjoyed it immensely. In fact, one of my biggest career regrets is that I did not start contracting earlier.

However, while there have been a number of challenges (which will be described later), the overall experience has been fantastic and I highly recommend it.

I have had a vast variety of work across different roles and industries, I have a much better work–life balance and I have also increased my earning power.

In general, I feel much happier and content with life.

Why Did I Want to Write This Book?

Over the past three or four years, I have mentored several individuals on contracting, interim management and freelancing. I have also performed lectures and workshops on contracting to various business schools, trade associations and industry bodies

Therefore, I thought it would be a good idea to combine this knowledge and experience into a single book, which can be shared and hopefully enjoyed by a much wider audience.

Therefore I really hope that this book helps you understand the world of contracting, interim management and freelancing – and more importantly whether it is suitable for you!

I hope you enjoy the read.

So You Want to Be a Contractor?

Why Do People Want to Become a Contractor?

I assume you are reading this book because you are thinking about making the jump to contracting.

Therefore, I would imagine that you are in a state of permanent employment, and you are unhappy with one or several aspects of it.

Poor Job Satisfaction

This could be caused by internal politics where you are spending more time 'playing games' than doing your job.

Poor Work–Life Balance

You are working long hours and do not have enough time off.

Poor Salary

You are unhappy with your remuneration. For example poor salary, no pay raises or having benefits being cut.

People Being Promoted above You

Maybe you have seen your fill of people being promoted above you even though they are not as talented as you.

Dull Work

The work itself is dull or not motivating

No Career Progression

There is no real prospect of intellectual growth or career progression.

Being Promoted Away from Your Job

People sometimes get promoted away from their preferred job.

For example, as a top accountant or good software programmer, you may be good at your job and enjoy it. However, because you are good at your job, you tend to get promoted up the management chain which means you move away from what you are doing.

Therefore your job satisfaction drops and you become unhappy.

Being Made Redundant from Permanent Work

With the increased number of redundancies over the past decade, there are a growing number of people going contracting because they either do not want to go back to permanent work or they are actually struggling to find permanent work.

No doubt there are several other reasons which I have not listed.

However if you answered "Yes" to any of the reasons above then I would strongly recommend that you investigate whether contracting is suitable for you.

Why Do Firms Want Contractors?

Despite what one reads in the media, contractors are very much in demand.

Firms will recruit contractors because they have a skill gap and also because they can be recruited and removed much easier and quicker than permanent staff.

Contractors will be used in a variety of situations. A few are listed below:

Specialist Skills.

To provide specialist skills that the firm does not have or only needs for short period of time. Such as tax accountancy, specific training or skills in a specific technology

Interim Management

To provide interim management skills. For example a manager has left and a contractor is brought in to bridge the gap while a permanent replacement is recruited.

Change/Project Management

To provide specific skills to support a project or change programme. For example project management, business analysis or technology skills.

Company Expansion

To support a company expansion. For example a firm is expanding but is worried about the financial risk of recruiting permanent staff. Therefore contractors are brought in initially because they can be recruited and removed at short notice.

Company Downsizing

To support a company downsizing. For example a firm is downsizing and contractors are brought into 'plug' skill gaps due to downsizing. Contractors can be recruited and removed at short notice.

Who Would Be Your Competition?

Competition would come from several areas.

Other Contractors

The most obvious would be other contractors who would be after the same roles. Therefore your competitive advantage would be driven by your skillset, rate, availability and as well as your ability to sell yourself through your CV and any interview process. (This is discussed further on in this book).

Larger Consultancy Firms

The other area of competition is from larger consultancy firms who are brought in to complete a project or piece of work.

These firms tender to go for the bigger pieces of work because they can bring a team of people onsite to complete work. Also it is sometimes easier for a client to 'outsource' the work to a single firm as opposed to recruiting and managing several individual contractors.

However it is not uncommon for contractors to actually be recruited to work for the larger consultancy firms to 'plug' any skill gaps they have. With the exception of the larger firms, most consultancies have a small set of permanent employees (say the owners, subject matter experts and administration staff). They then use contractors (or associates to use the correct term) to 'pad' out their teams for client projects. The advantage for the client is that they get a good team. The advantage for the consultancy firm is that they obtain decent staff that can be added or removed quickly. The advantage to us contractors is that we get some interesting work and normally at a decent rate of pay.

Permanent Staff at Client Sites

The final area of competition is the permanent members of staff at the client where we are working. It is not uncommon for existing permanent staff to hold some bitterness against contractors because they perceive them to be getting the more interesting work and being paid better. Therefore it is important that you build relationships with the permanent staff through doing a good job, working hard, delivering and being tactful

Changing Nature of Employment

As a side note, it is worthwhile to consider the changing nature of employment.

When I started working in 1980s, the focus was on getting a good permanent job. Because I lived near London, I was told to get a job with a bank or some large financial services organization. If you did well and kept your hand 'out of the till' then you could have a job for life.

However, as people know, things have changed since then. The world is more volatile and unstable. For example, the financial crisis in the late 2000s and Brexit in the EU and the UK

Therefore, firms do not want to employ vast amounts of staff as they did previously. This is because these are fixed costs which are hard to manage against a variable and unreliable external market.

Therefore this means there is an increased demand for contractors.

Millennials and Looking Forward

In additional the millennial generation has a different attitude towards work than older generations.

Millennials are very much more focused on a work–life balance. They are more than happy to move jobs more frequently. They would like much more flexibility, either in working from home or taking career breaks.

Therefore this means the structure of employment is actually moving toward a more freelance or contractor basis.

This means many people will probably move into freelancing or contracting even if they had no previous plans to do so.

Key Points

- There are a variety of reasons to 'make the jump'; such as (a) poor job satisfaction, (b) poor work-life balance, (c) poor work (d) no prospects going forward and (e) being promoted away from your job.

- Freelancers, contractors and interim managers are very much in demand.

- The main areas of competition are (a) other contractors, freelancers and interim managers (b) larger consultancy firms although contractors could end up working for them and (c) permanent members of staff where you are working.

- The changing nature of work and of the general population (e.g. millennials) is making freelancing, contracting and interim management more popular.

What Is It Like Being a Contractor?

There are some good points which are explained below. However (and to add some sort of balance to the argument) I have also described some drawbacks.

The Good Points

Control over Your Destiny

You have more control over own destiny. This is often one of the main reasons people go contracting.

It is important to note that while you have more flexibility than when you are working for a permanent employer, you do have to fit around clients' needs and demands (such as project deadlines).

Increase Earning Power

Contractor rates are definitely higher than permanent salaries and bonuses. However please note that you will have to pay for your own pension, holidays, sick pay and other expenses.

Also and it may sound obvious but if you do not work then you do not get paid.

However, working for yourself should give you further earning opportunities such as part time roles, directorships etc. and the move to a more portfolio career structure. (This is discussed in more detail below).

As a word of caution, if the only reason you are looking to become a contractor is to be rich and earn lots of money then this is probably the wrong reason. You will end up chasing the pound which will no doubt result in highly paid work (which is nice) but this work could be horrible. For example, working for an unpleasant client, working away from home for long periods of time, etc. Therefore you should ideally pick work that you enjoy and in circumstances that you are happy with.

More Interesting Work

Contracting opens up a greater variety of interesting work.

Personally, I have worked on a number of different projects covering:

- Operating model design
- Product design and launch
- Outsourcing
- Offshoring
- Business change
- Technology change and management
- Regulatory/Legal changes

I have also worked across a number of different industries; such as:

- Financial services
- Oil and gas
- Charities
- Professional bodies
- Trade associations

Therefore a range of different and interesting work.

Contracting has also allowed me to move towards a portfolio career – i.e. having a number of smaller jobs that add up to one single big job.

I have provided consultancy for several start-up social enterprises (covering areas such as gambling addiction awareness and the performing arts).

I have also picked up a few director roles.

I have also been the Chair of a national professional trade body focused on improving the standards of management within the UK.

I have also written a large amount. This covers textbooks on financial services and management (as well as this book). I have also written articles covering subjects such as Financial Services, Change Management, Internet-of-things and Big Data.

Finally I have managed to perform a number of lectures on entrepreneurship, career guidance, change management, and ethical management.

It Is Easier to Leave If It Is Not Working Out

As a contractor, it is much easier to leave a firm, than a permanent member of staff, if you do not like working there.

This can be done in one of two ways.

- You can decide not renew at the end of your current contract
- You could actually resign during the contract.

   Termination periods for contract work are usually shorter than for a permanent role. Normally 2 to 4 weeks where as permanent notice periods can be several months.

   However is not that common for a contractor to terminate during a contract.

Therefore if you do this then I would tread carefully. Your client will not be happy especially if you have left them in a bad position (such as half way through a project). You do not want to get a reputation for leaving clients in a difficult position because it could hinder you getting future work.

Obviously this is a double edged sword because the client could always terminate you early as well.

Gaps between Contracts and Assignments

It is unlikely that you will leave one contract on one day and then start your next contract the following day.

Therefore there will be 'natural' gaps between contracts. This can be used for resting, going on holiday, recharging your batteries, self-development, etc.

However some people do find these gaps scary because they are worried that the next contract may not turn up.

No More (Or Reduced at Least) Office Politics

Another good point of contracting is no more (or at least reduced) office politics. You do not have to play internal games and you can just get on with the job.

Improved Work-Life Balance

Contracting also allows an improved work–life balance.

This is a very common reason people make the jump. (It is one of the reasons that I made the jump).

While you are working for clients, you tend to be very busy. For example, on a recent assignment I was working fourteen hour days for six months. However when the contract was finished, I took some time off to rebalance my work life balance.

The Bad Points

Gaps between Assignments

If you would find the gaps between roles scary or unsettling then contracting is probably not for you. For example you do not like the fact you are not getting paid or you are worried that the next contract will not turn up.

Some people like the permanent feel of stability even if they are not particularly happy with the job they are doing.

Work Often Arrives At Short Notice

You often get work at short notice.

Several times, I have had an interview on one day and then been asked to start the next day often on a long-term contract.

People can find this immediate start time quite unsettling because it does not provide sufficient time to 'get emotionally ready' for a new role.

No Sick Pay, Holiday Pay, Pension, Insurance, etc.

Another thing to consider is the need to pay for your own pension, sick leave, holiday and insurance.   This needs to be factored into your fee.

Overheads of Running Your Own Company

Most contractors or freelancers have some sort of legal structure.

The overheads of running a business can be costly. Accountants, tax advisors, etc. are required which can be expensive.

Likewise it can be very laborious actually running the business. For example book keeping, performing annual returns, keeping track of receipts, etc.

(This entire area is discussed in much more detail later in the book).

Keeping Your Skills Up-To-Date and Relevant

While some clients may occasionally pay for training this is very uncommon.

Therefore it is up to you to keep your skills up-to-date; and to ensure they match your client needs,

This will require you to dedicate time and spend some money.

The Constant Need to Look for Work

As a contractor, one must constantly keep looking for work.

Even when you are in an assignment, you will need to constantly keep networking to ensure people know your situation and when you become available.

This can be a tiring process and laborious if one is not suited to it.

(This area is discussed in more detail later in this book).

No Management Progression

As a contractor, there is no management or career progression in the traditional sense.

While some contracts may include management roles (such as an interim management) or a senior change roles (such as a project or programme manager) there is very little management progression.

Therefore if you want to climb the management ladder, then contracting is probably not for you.

Remember Your Personal Situation

And the last, often forgotten area is a personal situation.

Obviously, everyone's personal situation is unique.

However, if you have a young family or a large mortgage then this will eat up a lot of money and stress. Therefore you may feel you need the stability of a permanent job.

Key Points

There are a number of good points:

- Flexibility (although there are always client demands)

- Increase earning power. However be aware if this is your main motivation because this is a poor reason to go contracting

- Exposure to more interesting work as well as work outside your normal sphere (such as directorships, writing, etc.)

- It is easier to leave a contract if you are unhappy (although this is a double edged sword because the client are remove you just as quickly)

- There are gaps between contracts (although some people do find these gaps unsettling)

- No more (or at least reduced) office politics

- A better work life balance

There are also a number of bad points:

- People can find the gaps between assignments scary. If this is the case then contracting or freelancing may not be for you!

- Work often arrives at short notice

- No sick pay, no holiday pay, no pension, no insurance, etc.

- Overheads of running your own company can be costly and laborious

- Keeping your skills up-to-date and relevant

- No management progression. If this is the case then contracting or freelancing may not be for you!

Finally remember your personal situation. If your personal circumstances (such as young family) require stability then contracting may not be for you (yet)!

Preparing to Go Contracting

Before you can make the jump there are a number of preparation activities that need to be done (although of course these can be done in parallel).

Do Research On Your Industry

This is important and time needs to be spent on this.

Do some research on how contracting works in your industry and in area of expertise.

Each industry will operate differently. Contracting in Financial Services operates very differently to contracting in (say) the Government or Oil/Gas industries. Likewise contracting for software developers is very different to contracting as an accountant.

It is important that you do not rush into contracting without understanding how your industry or area of expertise works because you could make some mistakes which could take a while to address.

However there are a vast number of sources of data that could be used.

- The best source of data is people who either are contracting now or have contracting in the past. They will have lived the dream (or nightmare). Therefore do not be afraid to speak to them and ask them questions.

    You will be surprised by how many people are willing to spend time helping you and answering questions.

- Additionally there are various books in the market (like this one) that provide hints and tips on contracting.

- Likewise there are a massive number of articles on the internet and in trade journals. They provide advice and opinions on all areas of contracting from "why to do it?" to "getting your first contract" to "to setting up your company" and so on.

- Post messages on social media (such as LinkedIn) asking any specific questions you have. Within LinkedIn there various specialist groups which are focused on contracting. If you post a question then somebody will nearly always reply.

- There are various webinars on contracting covering a wide of areas. It may beneficial to attend and / or listen into these.

- Also understand that there is a seasonable movement within contracting which will impact how easy or hard it is to find work.

  From my experience December, January and February are slow due to holidays and therefore it is hard to find work.

  March, April and May tend to be busier.

  However things slowdown in June, July and August due to the summer holidays before speeding up for September, October and November.

- Finally various organisations (such as trade bodies) or experienced individuals will perform presentations on going contracting. These can either be face-to-face or over the internet. Therefore it may be worthwhile attending a few to gather some insights.

Therefore just to iterate the point above. It is important to think, think, and think again before making the jump. Otherwise, you could be making a bad or hasty decision.

Do You Have Sufficient Experience?

Again before you make the jump to contracting, it is important to ensure that you have sufficient experience to make the jump.

Over my lifetime, I have seen a number of people make the jump too early without sufficient experience, which has caused problems down the line. People either cannot get work. Or if they do get work then it is poorly paid, working for challenging clients or end up working away from home for long periods of time.

Therefore, it is important to look yourself in the mirror and ask yourself, "Do I have sufficient experience to actually make a living being a contractor?"

This means it is advisable to have some sort of grounding in your industry before making the jump. Therefore it is important to have worked for a number of years in your industry to ensure you have sufficient experience of both your industry and area of expertise.

Preparing to Make the Jump

Now you have done your research and you are happy you have sufficient experience then you need to look at the following.

Understand What Your Skill Set Is

It is very important that you understand what your skill set is or, in other words, why would somebody want to employ you as a contractor?

Therefore be very specific about what you are offering. It should cover the following:

- Hard or technical skills. For example JAVA programmer, accountant or project manager

- Soft skills. For example ability to deal with challenging situations / people or the ability to deal with complexity

Typically I would recommend you limit this to no more than 20 words. While this is could be a challenge, it will ensure that your key selling point(s) is focused, sharp as well as easy to read and understand.

Some examples are as follows:

- "Project Manager with a successful record dealing with large enterprise-wide change"

- "Accountant with experience of dealing with complex tax arrangements across national borders"

It will also be good to do something you are good at and enjoy otherwise it will be hard to motivate yourself.

Build a Cash Buffer

An important item is to ensure that you have a cash buffer before you make the jump.

This is because it could take a while to get a piece of work and / or get your first invoice paid. This buffer will provide some protection against this and allow you to pay your bills, mortgages, etc.

The size of your cash buffer really depends on a person's own circumstances. Somebody with a large young family and/or large mortgage will require a bigger buffer than somebody with no dependent children with no or a small mortgage.

Personally, I went for a three-month buffer.

It is important to note that building this cash buffer can take a while. Therefore it may be necessary to skip holidays, have a less expensive Christmas or wait to upgrade that mobile phone because that will free up cash.

This requires some dedication and focus, but it will be short-term pain, hopefully to be replaced by long-term gain for going freelance contracting.

Understand How You Will Get Work

It is important to understand who will be your clients and how you will be able to access them.

One of the most common routes is using agencies. When the end-client needs a contractor then they will engage an agency to search the market for relevant candidates. If a candidate is successful then they will be employed by the end-client through the agency with the agency taking a cut for their efforts. This cut is normally a percentage of your fee.

There are a large number of agencies in existence each with a different focus. For example project managers, accountants, script writers and so on. Therefore it is important to understand which agencies are the most suitable for your industry and expertise. This could be found in the ways listed earlier (e.g. social media, forums, etc.) but I strongly recommend speaking to contractors in the same areas as yourself to determine which agencies are the best and which need to be avoided.

A second way is to go directly to the end-client. This will almost definitely get you the best work and rates (because there is no agency taking a cut) but this does require a large network of contacts which does take time (often years) to build. Therefore this route is most common with experienced contractors who have spent years building their networks.

A third area (which is becoming more and more common) is for consultancies to employ contractors. Effectively you will be branded as one of the consultancies staff (and often known as an "associate"). The advantage is that you will often get great, challenging and interesting roles because these consultancies often get the best work because of their extensive networks. The drawback is that the consultancy will take a cut of your fee and the number of these roles is lower than the other options. However, once you are in on the consultancy's list and you have done a good job then they will often re-use you so it could be a source of constant business.

Fourthly it is always possible to publicise your abilities on trade or specialist websites. However, from experience, this is only good for very specialist pieces of work. For example mentoring, public speaking, etc.

The final route is the end-clients contacting you and asking them to work for them. In effect a word-of-month or reputational recommendation. This is obviously the best way because people are approaching you as opposed to you looking for work. However this route will take time to build because you will need to have completed a large number of successful assignments to allow your reputation to grow. (There is more on creating and maintaining a good reputation later in this book).

What Rate Should I Charge?

Let us look at what you should charge for your work.

The key focus is ensuring you generate sufficient income to make a living – i.e. pay your bills, have some money to speak on leisure and continue to contribute to your savings.

The way you charge often depends on the type of work you are doing. But there are two common methods.

- The most common is area a day rate – i.e. you charge £XYZ pounds for each day. This is obviously easier for you to manage but some clients can get nervous because contractor costs could easily overrun.

- The second way (which is far less common) is to charge a fixed cost per project or item of work.

  For some pieces, this is fine but it tends to be around pieces of work that are easily scoped. For example taking a set of wedding photographs, running a training course or doing a firm's year-end tax accounts.

  However for anything that is not easily defined then you will need to use a scope document to confirm what exactly needs to be delivered with change request procedures to manage any changes to scope.

  For massive projects run by large suppliers (such as building an oil ring or constructing a new shopping centre) then this is fine because these large suppliers will have the people, money and skills to manage this. However for a small one man band contractor it is too risky and complex. Therefore I always tend to stay away from that and go down the day rate route.

On the assumption you have decided to charge a daily rate then you need to determine what actual rate you should charge?

This needs to be looked at from two angles:

- What you need to charge to ensure you have sufficient income to cover your expenses, pay yourself a salary and (hopefully) top up your cash buffer for a rainy day

- What the market and potential clients are willing to pay for your services

Regarding the first bullet point, you need to determine what you outgoings will be.

This will cover your salary, any dividends, and costs for running your company (such as accountant costs, tax, web hosting, business cards, insurance, etc.).

Once this is done then you need to estimate how many days a year you are likely to work by taking into account your holidays, public holidays, gaps between contracts and likely sick days.

Then you divide one into the other calculate your daily rate. For example, if you annual costs are

£80,000 and you plan to work 200 days per year then your minimum day rate is £400.

Regarding the second bullet regarding what the market or potential clients will pay. This is fairly hard to answer because it depends on your industry, skill set and the general economic climate. However it should be possible to search the internet to find the going rates across your industry. Also, if you use an agency, then they will be able to let you know what clients are willing or not willing to pay.

In an ideal world your demands and the market's demand will be very similar.

If there is a difference (i.e. you want more than a client is willing to pay) then you need to make a decision to either wait until a suitably paid contract arrives (which will use up your cash buffer) or go with the lower rate and watch your expenses.

Sort Out Your Pension

While the author is not suitably skilled (or regulated!) to give pension advice, I would strongly suggest you have a pension. Not unless, of course, you intend to work until you die?

This is a very tricky subject and the approach you take will be dictated by a number of factors; such what legal structure you use, your age when you want to retire and your existing pension arrangements.

Therefore I would strongly suggest you visit to a suitably skilled advisor to get some proper advice.

Where to Work

If your clients are local to you (or within a daily commute) then that is good.

However if they are not then are you prepared to work away from home for an assignment?

Some people do not like working away especially if they have a young family, other local commitments or generally like sleeping in their own bed at night.

However it is common for contractors to work away from home for often long periods of time. For example leave your house on Monday, return on Friday and use the weekend to do your washing before return on the Monday.

Some firms will allow you to work from home but others do not. In fact some firms have a policy of not allowing contractors to work from home at all. Therefore if you work away then plan for working away for the entire week.

Also remember to be 100% clear on who pays for travel and accommodation. For example does the client pay or do you pay? If you pay then do you include it in your rate or charge it on top as an expense?

Write a High Impact and Targeted CV

A good CV is essential to getting your first (or any) assignment.

Personally, I tend to look at a CV as a personal brochure. It will not get me an assignment (although a bad one will stop me getting work) but it will get me to the next stage of the process (i.e. the interview).

Therefore a CV should be relevant to the assignment that is being applied for. It would be a shame for you to have lots of experience and knowledge but not get a glance because your CV is poor or irrelevant.

A CV should have five main sections and should not be longer than 4 pages; namely:

- Personal details – covering your name, address, email and telephone numbers

- A statement about yourself – e.g. "A Change Manager with over 25 years delivering change in the Oil/Gas Industry"

- A list of jobs or previous assignment in reverse data order

- List of relevant qualifications.

- List of interests especially if they are relevant to the job. For example pro bono or NED experience

There are various websites and companies that charge for providing assistance in writing CVs.

While these tend to be good, do not be afraid to ask colleagues or people you know for their feedback. As I have said before, you will be surprised by how many people are willing to help.

Depending on the role or assignment that you are applying for then it may be necessary to tailor your CV for that role. For example stress a particular skill if it is relevant. While this requires more work, it will give you a much bigger chance of getting the assignment.

Learn Great Interview Skills

To be successful, you will need to learn great interview and self-selling skills.

I tend to look at interviews as a two-way process.

First, the client is interviewing you. They want to understand that you have sufficient skill and competence for the role.

Second, you can assess whether you want to work for that client. For example would you actually be able to work with the individuals who interviewed you? If not, then do you really want to pursue the work?

Interviews come in a variety of different formats. At one extreme they could be a very formal process where you meet at the client's site and have various interviews. In fact, for one assignment, I had had four interviews. At the other extreme, I have had interviews which lasted 15 minutes in a local coffee shop.

Regardless of the interview's format, the actual techniques are the same; viz:

- Before the interview, if possible, speak to industry colleagues about the client and the people interviewing you to see what they are like. This will provide some valuable inside information to help your preparation.

- Do some preparation on what questions you are likely to be asked and have answers ready. However you should make sure those answers do not sound too rehearsed. Otherwise it could look like you are reading from a script.

- Research your client so you can actually ask them appropriate questions regarding them and the job. It is important that you do ask question to (a) prove to the client you have taken an interest and (b) ensure you fully understand the role.

- Plan your journey for the interview (covering location, parking, or public transport). The last thing you want to do is turn up late, out of breath, sweaty or, even worse, at the wrong location.

- It is important to dress appropriately. This is a very tricky area. People have various views on this. As a general rule is never really a problem to overdress but it could be a problem if you underdress. Therefore I would also suggest dressing smartly.

- Always be pleasant and friendly. Lots of smiles and happy body language.

- When you leave the interview, always end on a high note with a hearty handshake and say, "Thanks."

If you have not attended an interview for a while then please take some time to learn interview skills

Practice does make perfect so do not be afraid to ask people to practice with you. It does feel odd but it is useful.

What Is Your Legal Set-Up?

To operate as a contractor, you need to set-up yourself up as some sort of legal entity.

There are four main types:

- Umbrella company

- Your own limited company

- Sole Trader

- Short term PAYE contract

Traditionally, nearly all contractors go down the Umbrella Company and/or Own Limited Company options. Very few (if any) have taken the Sole Trader option.

The main driver is who your client is happy or willing to engage with.

In all my years of contracting, I have not encountered a single client who is willing to engage with a Sole Trader. They have all insisted on employing me through either Umbrella Company or my own Limited Company.

Therefore I (like nearly all contractors) went down Umbrella Company or Own Limited Company routes.

However your situation could be different so I cannot really recommend anything solid here.

Using an Umbrella Company

An umbrella company is often offered by agencies and accountants. It works as follows:

- You are employed by the Umbrella Company which will employ a number of other contractors.

- The Umbrella Company will legally contract with your client or agent.

- This means the Umbrella Company will raise any invoices on your behalf and collect any monies from the client.

- The Umbrella Company will then pay you as a normal PAYE employee minus their fee.

There are some advantages to joining an umbrella company.

- They will look after your tax issues.

- They are quick to join (sometimes less than 2 days).

- They tend to be cheaper to operate than an Own Limited Company.

- You have limited liability.

However there are some disadvantages.

- It is less flexible because you are still employed by another firm.

- Also it will not be easy to have multiple streams of work.

- Finally you do not get any tax advantages such as paying yourself through a combination of PAYE salary and dividends.

Actually using an Umbrella Company is common for a new contractor starting out. They use an Umbrella Company initially while their own company is being set up. (This is exactly what I did).

Your Own Limited Company

The second option is owning your own company.

The main advantage is its flexibility; viz:

- You have limited liability.

- You can use the company for other things such as multiple work streams,

- You can pay yourself using a combination of PAYE and dividend (which gives some tax benefit).

- You can also use the company for other activities.

The disadvantage is that you have the overheads of running the company (such as employing an accountant) and you will be responsible for all company matters (such as tax, VAT, annual accounts, etc.).

Setting up your limited company can take some time and effort.

Firstly you need to get an accountant. There are literally hundreds of accountants available who specialise in small business and / or contractors. However it is a little daunting to select a suitable one. Therefore I would suggest speaking to other contractors for recommendations.

If you have selected an accountant then I would recommend you ask them to help with the set-up of the company. In fact some accountants may have some companies that you could buy 'off the shelf' from them.

However if you do need to set-up a company then the steps are as follows:

- Register your company name with Companies House who will check for any company with similar or same names. (It is common to use a combination of your initials or the children's names.

Although some people just use two random words together).

- Confirm the company's registered address. This will normally be your accountant's or your home address.

- Determine who the company's officers are. You will need at least one director (which will be you) although you could add a second (such as your spouse or partner). You will also need a Company Secretary (although this could be your accountant). For each of these named people, you will need their full name and address.

- Confirm the number of shares to be issued and who owns then. Typically 100 shares are issued which will be allocated to yourself. Although I have seen some companies with only 1 share.

- Determine whether your company needs to register for VAT. Basically if your income is over a certain threshold then you must (legally) register for VAT. I would recommend discussing this with your accountant. It is also possible to register for the VAT Flat-Rate scheme which could reduce your VAT payments in certain circumstances. Again I would ask your accountant about this.

Finally you need to open a bank account to receive invoice monies into and pay your expenses (such as salary) out of. Years ago this used to be a simple process but with the far more stringent Know-Your-Client demands this could take a while because the bank will need to perform a large number of checks on you as the key director.

Sole Trader

The other option is as a sole trader.

The advantage here that it is cheap and easy to set up. The disadvantage is your unlimited liability, which basically means you personally are responsible for all debts.

However, as mentioned earlier, a large number of clients will not employ you if you work as a sole trader.

Short term PAYE contract

This arrangement is similar to a normal PAYE employment contract except that is a clear defined end clause in place. This could be a specific date or when a set of pre-defined tasks or projects have been completed. This differs from normal PAYE contracts whose end-date is triggered by the action of either the employer or employee; for example a resignation, a dismissal or redundancy. Under a fixed term contract then employees should have the same benefits as normal employees. For example equivalent pay, employment benefits and protection from redundancy.

Ensure You Have the Correct Insurance in Place.

It is necessary to ensure you have sufficient insurance in place. In fact most clients (or agents) will not employ you unless you have this in place.

There are three types:

- Professional Indemnity. This covers you against financial loss to your client for your mistakes or poor advice.

- Public Domain. This covers you if you accidentally cause an accident on the work place; such as somebody trips over you, gets injured and then claims against you.

- Employer's Liability. This is only needed if you have employees. This is unlikely if you are contracting but you never know. Although this type of insurance is often covered under Professional Indemnity and / or Public Domain policies.

It is a tricky to give advice on the amount of insurance to take out. It really depends on your client, your agent and their needs. Therefore, when starting an assignment, you should ask them what the client want.

As always, I would recommend shopping around for the best prices and cover but (as previously suggested) I would check with your fellow contractors to see what insurers they use.

Setting Up Your Web Site

While this is not 100% necessary (because professionals will often use LinkedIn and Twitter for their on-line presence) I would recommend have some sort of web-site. It will increase your exposure and it is relatively simple and cheap to set-up and maintain.

There are four main stages:

- Registering a domain name
- Hosting the site
- Designing the site
- Maintaining the site

With regard to registering the domain name. There are a large number of firms that will register your domain name (e.g. www.NAME.co.uk). A simple internet search (or asking other contractors) should find a suitable firm. However it is important to ensure you register as many suffixes as possible (i.e. www.NAME.com, .co.uk, .org.uk, etc.). This will ensure you have maximum usage over the name.

Once you have registered your domain name then you need to find somebody to host the site.

Again there are several firms who will do this (including almost definitely the firm who registered your domain name). Per above a simple internet search (or checking with other contractors) will find a suitable firm. There are number of factors that I would look at when selected a firm to host.

These will cover items such as:

- Cost
- Availability of site
- Support in the event of problems
- On-line tools for creating / maintaining the site
- Ability to add blogs
- Ability to collect payments
- Ability to receive emails

Now you have your domain name and found a firm to host it then you need to actually design the website. If the hosting firm has an on-line tool to create pages then this should be much easier.

My rule-of-thumb when design web sites is 'keep it simple' or 'less is more'. Nothing turns people off more than complex and hard to use websites.

Therefore your site should have:

- A simple logo
- An (up-to-date) picture of yourself

- A summary of your skills (taken from your CV)

- Email contact detail – I would not include a telephone number just in case you get inundated with a large number of crank calls

- Links any other applicable sites (such as your LinkedIn profile, any publications you have published and so on)

Now you have your website and running it is important to maintain it on a regular basis. I would suggest reviewing it every four weeks to see if any changes are required (such as updating your skill sets).

LinkedIn Profile

This social media site is used heavily in the contracting (and general business) world. It is not uncommon for clients and agents to view contractor's LinkedIn profiles to see their background and who they know before arranging interviews and offering assignments.

Therefore it is essential your LinkedIn profile is up-to-date and valid; viz:

- Ensure there is suitable (and up-to-date) photo of you.

- Ensure your headline is relevant; e.g. Consultant with experience of implementing technology change.

- Ensure your job history is up-to-date and it matches your CV.

- Ensure you have sent invites to all your key contacts. This should give the impression you are well connected.

- Ask for recommendations (especially) from senior and important people from previous jobs. This should add gravitas to your profile.

- Ensure any other achievements (such as qualification, publications, etc.) are included and they match what is on your CV.

Email Signature

Ensure your email signature is up-to-date and reflects that you are contracting.

Apart from your name, I would include your LinkedIn URL, twitter address and email address. I would not include a telephone number just in case you get inundated with a large number of crank calls.

Business Cards

Business Cards seem to be going out of fashion at the moment. However they are key tool when networking; i.e. at the end of discussion you can hand over your business card as a departing gift.

Therefore I would recommend having some printed. Again you should be able to find a suitable firm by a quick internet search or by asking other contractors for suitable printer.

Stationery

While most communication these days is electric (such as email and text messaging), you will need some letter headed stationery primarily for your invoices and for any other official letters you may need to write.

Therefore it is best to have something prepared. It does not need to be too fancy. It just needs to contain your company name (and logo) and registered address details. It should be possible to create something on MS-Word or a similar package.

Other Marketing Materials

As a contractor you are unlikely to require any formal marketing materials (such as a brochure or presentation banner).

However it may be useful to have some case studies available which can be printed off, emailed and/or posted on your web-site or Linkedin profile. If written correctly then they can be a good advert for your skills. (One word of caution: if you do write case studies then be careful with any client confidentiality issues).

Key Points
Do some research on how your industry

operates otherwise you could be make a mistake that is costly and time-consuming to address.

Ask yourself do you have sufficient experience to go contracting? It is advisable to have some sort of grounding in your industry before making the jump.

Now you have done your research and you are happy you have sufficient experience then you need to look at the following:

- Understand what your skill set is? I.e. why would somebody want to hire you as a contractor?

- Build a cash buffer. This will provide protection in the first months of running when getting work and your first invoices paid

- Understand how you will get work. The most common route are through agencies but there are other routes such as direct to the clients, through consultancies, trade press and word-of-mouth.

- Understand how you will charge - e.g. daily rate (which is most common) or a fixed rate per project.

- Understand what rate you will charge. The rate should cover your outgoings (taking into account periods when you will not work) and match what the industry is willing to charge for your skill set.

- Understand how going contracting will impact your pension. Therefore speak to an advisor to get some proper guidance.

- Are you willing to work away from home for periods of time? If so then understand who will pay your travel and accommodation.

- Write a great CV. Remember it may be necessary to tailor your CV for individual assignments.

- Learn interview skills. Remember this is a two way process. The client is interviewing you and you are interviewing to determine whether you want to work there.

- Ensure you have the most relevant legal set up. There are three types; namely Umbrella, Limited Company and Sole Trader.

- Ensure you have insurance in place. There are three types; public domain, professional indemnity and employer liability. Your client and / or agent will often dictate what insurance is required.

- (While not 100% necessary) I would suggest have a simple but focused website.

- Ensure your LinkedIn profile is up to date.

- Ensure your email signature reflects you

are a contractor.

- Produce some business cards. They are ideal for networking.

- Produce some headed stationery (for your invoices and any other formal documents).

  Formal marketing documentation is not 100% necessary but some case studies on previous work is good. However be aware of any client confidentiality issues.

IR35 – Update on the changes being made

Background

Originally this section on IR35 was part of the previous chapter ("Preparing to go Contracting") but considering the possible material changes being made to IR35 then I decided to create a dedicated chapter on it. Anyway before we drop into the detail of this area, I need to stress that this section is a summary of IR35 and its likely implications. It is not meant to provide legal or tax guidance. As I have stressed in other parts of this book, please always get proper external advice on these matters.

IR35 is a UK tax regulation. It was launched in 2000 and was designed to close a loop-hole where contractors can create their own limited company to filter payments through to pay less tax by using a combination of PAYE and dividends. The loop hole related to 'disguised employees' who are contracting in "name and structure" but effectively a long term employee. For example a contractor has been working for the some client, doing the same job for many years. In fact in some cases longer than some permanent employees

If one is caught by IR35 then they are taxed as an employee and not a contractor. Although one is unlikely to get access to other benefits that full-time employees have such as holiday entitlement, sick pay, pension contributions and so on.

IR35 introduced two key terms (namely "inside IR35" and "outside IR35") which need to be understood.

- If you are "inside IR35" then you are considered an employee for tax reasons. This means you will pay taxes (namely National Insurance Contributions and Income Tax) at the same rate as other equivalent employees. This tax payment is called the "deemed payment" and it will be made by the organisation who pays you. This organisation is called the "fee payer" and could be your client or recruitment agency.

- If you are deemed "outside IR35" then you are considered self-employed for tax reasons and you can pay yourself in a tax efficient way (such as using a combination of PAYE and dividends through your own limited company

Recent reforms in 2017 and 2020.

While the legislation has been live for many years, the UK Government was still not happy because they felt many contractors were still abusing the system.   Hence a number of reforms are being rolled out.

Originally contractors used to determine whether they were inside or outside of IR35 (and, for obvious reasons, most contractors determined they were outside IR35.). Therefore changes are being rolled out to make the "fee payer" responsible for determining whether a contractor is in or out of IR35. The "fee payer" will also be responsible for paying any extra tax liability.

This changes were rolled out for the UK public sector in 2017 and they will be rolled out for private sector medium and larger organisations from April 2020.

Private sector small firms are currently exempt. If a contractor works for one of these firms then the contractor is still responsible for determining their IR35 status. A small firm is defined if an organisation does not exceed two of the following (a) more than 50 staff (b) balance sheet total of £5.1 million and/or (c) annual turnover of £10.2 million.

How does a "fee payer" determine whether you are in or out of IR35?

At the time of writing, there is no clear legal method to determine if a person is an employee or not. The legal methods employed are a combination of various court decisions and case law.

However the "fee payer" can assess IR35 status in two ways

- Firstly they can use the HMRC's "Check Employment Status for Tax" (CEST) tool to determine when a contract is in or out of IR35. CEST was introduced for the 2017 reforms but it has been heavily criticised for being too simplistic for such a complex area. (Even the HMRC have admitted that CEST is still work in progress)

- The other option is for the "fee payer" to perform their own assessment. This can either be done by their in-house team or by employing some external consultants. From the author's personal experience, this route appears to be the most common so far.

Regardless of the approach, the assessment will cover questions such as the following

- Does the contractor have their own business premises?

- Does the contractor employ other employees?

- Can the contractor who has been provided for the assignment be substituted for another suitable skilled individual who is working for the named company?

- Does the contractor have normal things for running their business? For example headed paper, a web site, business cards, personalised email addresses and so on.

- Does the contractor charge on a per hour basis? Or on a per project basis?

- How specific is the wording regarding the work provided? For example is a simply "Project Manager" or does it break down the work into scope, stages, phases, deliverables, etc. of the project being delivered.

- Is there any financial risk to the contractor if there are problems with the assignment?

- Is there an obligation for the "fee payer" to provide the contractor with work at all times?

- Does the "fee payer" have control over the work being carried out by the contractor?

- Is the contractor covered by the "fee payers" normal HR policies? For example staff appraisals, disciplinary procedures, grievance procedures, subsidised staff canteen, social events, holiday pay, sick pay, maternity / paternity pay, bonus payments, share options, pensions and so on.

- Is the contractor identifiable from permanent staff? E.g. different ID passes

- Does the contractor use their own equipment and materials?

- Does the contractor have other contracts and work orders with other "fee payers"?

- Plus many others

Once this assessment is completed then the "fee payer" will send the contractor a "Status Determination Statement" before work starts confirming whether they feel whether you are in or out of IR35. This statement will also document the decisions and reasons behind their ruling.

If you disagree with the ruling (i.e. they have deemed you inside IR35 but you feel you are outside IR35) then the contractor has the right to challenge the decision. If so then the "fee payer" has 45 days to respond either confirming their original decision or by providing a different status.

The decision to push the tax liability onto clients has proved challenging and frightening for many firms. In fact when the reforms were introduced for public sector employees in 2017 then the majority of public sector organisations issued blanket policies stating that all contractors were inside IR35 regardless of whether the contractor's situation meant they were in or not.

While it is impossible to predict what the private sector will do in 2020, it would not be surprising for large firms with large numbers of contractors to issue blanket statements that all contractors will be in IR35 regardless of their situation.

However only time will tell.

What is the impact to Contractors?

Firstly you need to determine what you feel your IR35 status is. The bullet points above should be able to help but I would strongly recommend getting some proper professional advice on this.

Once you understand your situation then you need to speak to your client(s) to understand their views and to determine their approach for assessing contractors for IR35. As mentioned above most public sector clients and large private sector organisations are taking the view that all contractors are inside IR35. However there will be many other clients who will take a different view especially if you can convince them that you are outside IR35.

Also as mentioned above, you can always challenge any decisions but the key point to remember is that the decision is the "fee payers" and not yours.

Therefore if you are not happy then the only recourse you have is leave the client and look for work elsewhere.

Summary

IR35 (like all employment law) is very complex. Also (the reformed) IR35 is new without any case law to provide direction. Therefore it will take a while for the rules and changes to 'bed in'.

Some people have said that IR35 could kill the contracting industry. However remember that many organisations will still require short-term workers (per the reasons in described earlier in this book) but they be employed via a short term PAYE arrangements as opposed via their own limited company.

Apologies for repeating myself but I want to stress that this section is a summary of IR35 and its likely implications. It is not meant to provide legal or tax guidance. Please always get proper external advice on these matters.

Key Points
IR35 is a UK legislation that has been live since 2000.
However reforms are currently being rolled out to force the "fee payer" (i.e. the client or

recruitment agency employing you) to determine whether you are "inside" or "outside" IR35. Previously the contractor could decide whether they are in or outside IR35.

If you are "inside" IR35 then will need to pay PAYE and make National Insurance contributions like a normal permanent employee.

If you are "outside" IR35 then you can you pay yourself using tax efficient methods such as a combination of PAYE and dividends.

These reforms were rolled out for UK public sector firms in 2016 and are due to be rolled out for UK medium and later organisations from April 2020. (At present small private sector firms are exempt).

Therefore it is important to understand your "fee payers" (i.e. client) approach on this so you can plan accordingly

A Key Point for a First Time Contractor

Now that all the preparation has been done, you now need to look for an actual contract. This subject is discussed in more detail in the next chapter but there is a key point for any first time contractor.

You May Need to Leave Your Permanent Job before Getting a Contract

This is a big step and most people are very nervous when making it (I know I was).

From my experience, clients will not normally wait for no longer than four weeks for a start date. The norm is that the client will want you to start as soon as possible after they make an offer.

Therefore if you have a permanent notice period longer than one month then you will almost definitely have to resign from your permanent role before securing your first or assignment.

This can be very unsettling (Personally I found it very unsettling).

However, if you have your cash buffer in place and have completed all the preparation work detailed in the earlier chapter then you should be fine.

(As a side note; when you leave your permanent role make sure you leave on good terms. This will ensure that you do not have a reputation for leaving firms in the 'lurch' which could stop you getting work in the future. Also they may need to provide a reference for you in the future. And if contracting does not work out, then you may want to go back there).

Key Points

As a first time contractor, you will possibly need to leave your permanent role before you have secured a contract if your notice period is longer than 4 weeks. This can be unsettling.

Looking for and Finding Contracts

Looking for a contract (whether it is your first or hundredth) is very similar to any job search.

Let the Market Know You Are Looking for Contract Work

This is a proactive process and you need to be determined.

You need to let the market know you are available for work.

- Send your CVs to any suitable agencies. While the initial approach could be an email, be warned that your email could go into a 'black hole' and be lost.

  Therefore I would also recommend ringing the agency and speaking to a 'real person' to ensure they have your CV, are reviewing it and considering you for opportunities.

- Likewise if you have any direct contacts at clients (such as previous managers and colleagues) then email them and then call them to ensure you speak to a 'real person'.

  Ask them have they any positions. Also ask them they aware of any positions in other organisations.

- Furthermore load your CV onto various job websites or job boards.

  I would also suggest keep re-loading your CV every few days. This is because agencies will often download the latest CVs every few days and you want to ensure that your CV is downloaded for review.

Apply for Roles

As well as loading your CV onto job boards, you also need to search the jobs listed and start applying.

(As mentioned earlier it may be necessary to tailor parts of your CV to bring out any key experiences or knowledge that will help with your application).

When you have applied for a role then ring the agency (or firm) who are running the recruitment process to speak to a 'real person' to learn more about the role (such as the rate, length of contract, location, skills required and any other details). Also you can ask them whether they feel you are a good fit and whether they will be taking your application forward. If not then you can ignore this application and move onto the others.

One the key dilemmas is if two (or more agencies) approach you about the same position – i.e. which agency do you choose because only one agent can represent you? While there are no hard and fast rules, I would always go with the agency who contacted me first even if the other agencies appear to offer a better rate or other benefits. First come first served.

Keep an activity log (or spreadsheet) of all the roles you have applied for so you can track and chase progress. Also you do not want to apply for the same role twice. It sounds strange but it does happen

Be Determined

Finally remember to be determined.

Do not expect to get a contract straight away. Keep pushing and chasing. This can be frustrating, hard work, and sometimes very demotivating, but remember this short-term pain will be balanced by the long-term gain of being a contractor.

The Interview or Selection Process

If the client likes your CV then they will invite you in an interview

The earlier chapter discusses interview skills in detail but I have summarised the key points below again for completeness.

- Interviews are a two-way process.

  First, the client is interviewing you because they want to ensure you have sufficient skills and competence for the role.

  Second, you can see whether you want to work for that client.

- Interviews come in a variety of different formats. At one extreme they could be a formal process where you meet at the client's site for a formal meeting; but at the other extreme, they could be chat over a coffee or even a telephone conversation.

- Regardless of the interview's format, the actual techniques are the same; viz:

  Before the interview, if possible, speak to people about the client and the people interviewing you to see what they are like and provide some valuable inside information to aid your preparation.

Research your client so you can actually ask them appropriate questions regarding the client and the job. It can prove that you have shown an interest in the client.

Plan your journey for the interview (for example) location, parking, or public transport so you do not turn up late, out of breath, sweaty or, even worse, at the wrong location.

Dress appropriately.

Do some preparation on what questions you're likely to be asked and have answers ready.

Always be pleasant and friendly.

When you leave the interview, always end on a high note with a hearty handshake and say, "Thanks."

After the interview, you should receive feedback reasonably quickly from the client which could cover anything from (a) they want to make you an offer (b) you were not suitable and will not be taken forward or (c) they have not made up their mind because they have other people to see. Sometimes they client may ask you to come back for another interview.

However this also gives you the opportunity to determine whether you want to continue with the application. If you do not like the client or role then do not be afraid to withdraw your application.

When You Are Offered a Contract

Once you have completed the application process, gone through the interview process then hopefully you will get an offer for a role.

Pre-Employment Checks

Before you are physically sent a contract to sign there is often a set of pre-employment checks required. (I appreciate that you are not a permanent member of staff but many firms will still insist on this).

Unfortunately these checks can be very thorough and tedious.

On a personal nature, firms will cover areas such as:

- References from previous employers

- Character references

- Criminal record checks

- Proof you can work in contract's location; such as proof you can work in the UK or in the EU

- Proof of qualifications such as certificates or award letters. (For one contract I had to supply copies of my O Level certificates from the mid-1980s)

- Any gaps in employment will need to be explained to prove that you were not up to 'no good'.

Therefore you may need to provide travel documents if you were abroad, bank statements to prove you did not have any income during that period and, sometimes, find somebody who is able to confirm you were not employed (or in prison) during that period.

In addition you will need to provide details on your company for verification. This could cover:

- Certificate of incorporation
- VAT certificate
- Bank details
- Bank statements
- Accountant details (you may have to confirm that you are you!)

From experience, I tend to keep an electronic folder containing all the types of documents required here so I can provide them quickly if required.

While it is tedious it is a necessary evil due to employment law and company policies.

Receiving, Reviewed and Signing the Contract

Once the above checks are completed (or sometimes almost complete) then you will be sent a contract.

Regardless of whether you are through an agency, direct to a client via a consultancy company then there will be some sort of contract you need to sign.

Remember from earlier in the book:

- If you use an agency then the contract will be between you (or your company) and agent. The agent will have a contract with the end client.

- If you are direct then you (or your company) will probably contract directly with the client. Although some firms will have an in-house to act as a legal buffer.

- If you going through a consultancy (as an associate) then the contract will be between you (or your company) and consultancy. The consultancy will have a contract with the end client.

Irrespective of the legal process, before signing, I would strongly recommending reviewing it in to ensure it reflects what was discussed during the application process; namely:

- Is the rate the same as discussed during the application process?

- Do you need to charge VAT?

- What is the start date? (Although this is often subject to any pre-employment checks. See earlier in this chapter).

- Is the length of the contract the same as discussed during the application process?

- What hours are you expected to work?

- Is the location the same as discussed during the application process?

- Are you happy with the role description and does it match what was discussed in the application process? For example Project Manager working on Project ABC.

- What is your notice period if you want to leave before the end of the contract?

- What is the clients' notice period if they want to terminate you before the end of the contract? (Note that is now more and more common for the client's notice period to be much shorter than your notice period. Say 2 weeks verses 4 weeks).

- What insurances are required? Remember the discussion in the previous chapter regarding public domain, professional indemnity and employer liability insurances.

- Is the situation regarding IR35 compliance? Again remember the discussion about this in the earlier chapter.

- What is the invoicing process for you to get paid? For example monthly sheets submitted within 5 working days after month end with you getting paid 20 working days after month end.

- You will also need to understand who owns the intellectual property of any work you perform. Normally the client will insist on owning everything you produce (like a normal permanent employee). However it is best to double check because you do not want to get in trouble for using a piece of software you developed for one client to another client.

If you are unhappy or unclear with any of the arrangements then it is important they are raised because once the contract is signed then it is very hard to change it.

Obviously the client, agent or consultancy may not be willing to change the contract for you.

If they will not change it and you are still unhappy then you will need to take a view on whether the issue is significant enough not to progress with the contract and role.

Finally most agency or consultancy contracts have some sort of 'lock in' or 'exclusivity' clause which means you cannot work for the end client for period of time (say three years) without going through the original agent or consultancy. Basically this is to protect the agent and consultancy from you working for the client for a short period of time, leaving and then re-joining immediately as a direct contractor and cutting them out of their fees.

Starting a Contract

Now the pre-employment checks are completed and the contract has been signed, you ready to start work.

Starting a contract role is not that different to starting a permanent or any other role.

You will be given a start date/time, a location and somebody to ask for.

Your first few days will cover meeting your new colleagues, attending various regulatory briefings, trying to log-on your PC, trying to find the toilets, getting a building pass, trying to work how the coffee machine works, etc.

However as an expensive contractor then you will be expected to get down to work immediately. Therefore you be thrown in at the deep end with reading, meeting key people and getting down to work.

This means you need to be a self-starter.

This can be uncomfortable but it comes with being a contractor. You will get used to it.

Key Points

Get your name out to the market and they e (i.e. clients, agencies and consultancies) know you are looking for work.

Start applying for roles. Always chase up roles and try to speak to a 'real person' to (a) understand more about the role and (b) whether you are suitable.

Be determined and persistent.

Some sort of interview will be required. Remember it is a two-way process. The client will be checking you as well as you checking out the client.

When offered a contract you have to perform pre-employment checks. This can be tedious but are essential.

Once you have received the actual physical contract then thoroughly check it and ensure it matches your expectations.

Starting a new contract is very similar to starting any role but as an expensive contractor you will be expected to get working immediately.

Day-to-Day Activities

Now that you have made the jump and you are working as a contractor then there are a number of activities you need to do on an ongoing basis.

Maintain and Protect Your Reputation

The first item of business is to protect your reputation.

Your reputation is arguably your biggest asset as a contractor.

While a large amount of work is through agencies and consultancies, most industries are very small and tight knit and it is amazing who knows who. This means there is a large amount of word-of-mouth recommendation. Therefore, if you have a good reputation, you will receive more work. If you have a bad reputation you will struggle.

Therefore how do you get a good reputation and then keep it?

- Do not let people down. Deliver what you promised and, if possible, try and over-deliver.

- Do not try to make other people look bad or at fault. Do not blame them for problems or set them up for failure. If they are having problems, feel free to help them out.

- Be open, honest and have high integrity. Delivering bad news is a key skill for a contractor. Do not try to hide problems and do not lie.

- Be nice and easy to work with. Be happy, be open, have good body language and be easy to contact (i.e. answer emails and telephone calls).

- Try to look professional. Dress smartly. If you have a rucksack, make sure it is not torn or with logos on it.

- Turn up on time.

Keep Your Skills Up to Date

It is important to ensure that you keep your skills up to date. Without stating the obviously, unless you have marketable skills then you will not pick up any work.

Therefore it is important to understand what skills are required by your clients and industry.

There are a number of ways to track this.

- The first way is to check with clients and try and understand what skills they require now and in the future.

- Also speak to agencies because they will know what skills their client are looking for.

- Speak to other contractors to see what they feel is required. Again, do not be afraid to ask because people will share information.

- Read the trade press and any relevant industry reports. They will provide details on where your industry is moving and therefore what skills you will need.

- Scan and review the various social media sites (such as LinkedIn and Twitter) because they will contain articles talking about the future of your industry and what skills will be needed.

It is important to bear in mind that these skills can be technical (such as tax accountancy or .NET programming) as well as soft skills (such as management, dealing with conflict, etc.).

Once you have determined which new or updated skills are required then you need to think about how to obtain them.

- You will pick up new skills (and experiences) when you are working in a contract as part of your day-to-day activities.

- Various business schools, colleges, universities and training companies run courses which you can attend. Some of these are virtual (or on-line) so they can be done out of hours but others may require you to attend an actual face-to-face lecture.

- You can read books (paper or electronic) to learn new skills. This can be published through traditional bookshops as well through industry and trade bodies.

- It is possible to learn from social media web-sites (such as LinkedIn and Twitter). There are a host of articles that provide some decent information.

- One other good route is looking at YouTube videos. There are a large number of good (and free) training videos covering a wide range of subjects.

- There are also a large number of webinars and seminars covering a wide range of subjects. These are very useful to attend to pick up new skills.

- Finally there are number of professional qualifications you can obtain such as PRINCE (for Project Management), ITIL (for Technology Service Management) and various accountancy qualifications.

Managing Your Business Affairs on a Day to Day Basis

It is important to manage your business on a day-to-day basis. This does not sound glamorous (and it is not to be honest). However it is essential you keep this under control because it could cause problems later down the line.

Raising Invoices and Tracking Them for Payment

It is essential that you issue invoices as soon as they are due. Again, without stating the obvious, if you do not raise and issue invoices then you will not get paid.

While an invoice is a key document, it does not need to be a complex document. It should cover the following:

- A unique identification number – e.g. INV-CLIENTA-001

- Your company name, address and contact information

- The name and address of the client for invoice is for

- A clear description of what you're charging for – e.g. 20 man days' effort for July 2017

- The date of the invoice

- The amount(s) being charged

- VAT amount if applicable

- The total amount owed – i.e. the total of the above two

- The date that payment is due

- Details on how to pay (e.g. your bank account details)

You should be able to create a simple template. However your accountant may create and issue invoices if you ask them.

It is important that you track invoices to ensure they are paid. Therefore I would create a simple tracking sheet containing the following columns:

- A unique identification number – e.g. INV-CLIENTA-001

- Client

- Details of work performed – e.g. 20 man days effort

- Amount (include VAT and other expenses)

- Date invoice sent

- Date payment due

- Number of days left to pay or number of days late (to allow tactful chasing)

- Date actually paid

- Flat VAT rate details (to allow this calculation to be made for your VAT return)

If invoices are late for payment then do not be afraid to chase for payment. Remember that it is your money!!

Pay People You Owe Money to

In similar manner to the above, if you owe people money for services (such as your accountant, website hosting, business cards, etc.) then pay them when due. If you do not pay them then they could withdraw their services which could cause you real issues.

However there is a growing trend for suppliers to put a standing order in place to ensure they get paid.

Manage Your Business Expenses (And Ensure They Are Genuinely Business Related)

As well as paying suppliers, you will have a number of general expenses which can be charged against your company.

You will need to check with your accountant regarding your specific list but the following provides starting point:

- Accountancy fees
- Advertising
- Bank Fees (including overdraft interest)
- Business Entertaining
- Capital Purchase (such as equipment)
- Computer Consumables
- Eye Test & Glasses
- Hotel Travel & Subsistence
- Insurance
- Internet Access
- Mobile phones
- Net Staff Payments
- Pensions
- Postage
- Printing & Stationery
- Professional Fees for the Company
- Reference books & Journals
- Rent of Business Premises
- Rent/Costs of additional home
- Staff Entertaining
- Telephone
- Training
- Travel - Car, Air, Taxi, Bus and other

It is important that if you charge an expense against your business then it is a genuine business expense.

For example; it should be possible to argue with the Tax Office that a JAVA programming course is a real expense if you are a software developer. However you may struggle to convince the Tax Office that a two week holiday in the West Indies is a business expenses.

The rule of thumb I use is 'if I was not working would I have incurred this expense?'

Finally keep detailed records for expenses as well as copies of all receipts. This will be used for your annual accounts. (See below).

Remember to Pay Yourself

Remember to pay yourself an income.

This could be split between PAYE and a dividend. Although I would check with your accountant regarding what (if any) split is possible. Years ago there were some good tax advantages of splitting your income but these days these advantages have been reduced to almost nothing.

Monitor and Manage Your Cash Position

Manage your cash very closely on a day-to-day basis.

As contractors are a one-man band, you need to monitor your money. You do not want to have problems due to a lack of money.

On a regular basis reconcile your bank statements against (a) any monies received in such as a payment for an invoice and (b) any monies paid out such as standing orders for suppliers.

Any errors or issues will need immediate investigation.

If you think you will go overdrawn (for whatever reason) then let the bank know as soon as possible to ensure you can put arrangements in place. Banks do not like surprise overdrafts and they may actually pull the plug if they are not comfortable.

Finally remember to monitor your cash buffer to ensure you constantly top it up to ensure you have sufficient cash to cover any emergencies (such as invoices paid late).

Regular Events That Need Management

There are a number of regular that will need addressing

Year End Accounts

If you are using your own limited company then you will need to complete a set of year end accounts.

(If you use an umbrella company then they will do their own accounts because you are effectively an employee of them. If you are a sole trader then you report through your personal tax return).

The actual collation of the accounts will need to be done by your accountant however they will you to provide all the input data, viz:

- Invoices raised
- Invoices raised but not yet paid
- Any other income (such as bank interest)
- Expenses paid
- Expenses due but not yet paid

This re-enforces the point of keeping good, accurate and up-to-date records.

Once the accounts are completed then you (as the main director) will need to review and sign them off.

Once this is done then the accountant will submit them to the HMRC so you can pay your Corporate Tax bill (see below).

Corporate Tax (For Own Limited Company Only)

Any corporate tax needs to be paid within nine months of your company year end. Your accountant will calculate the amount required but you (as a Director) will be responsible for making the actual payment to the HMRC.

Pay-As-You-Earn (PAYE) Returns

Employers are responsible for calculating employee's National Insurance and Income Tax and then paying it to the HMRC.

If you use an umbrella company then they will be responsible and will you have to do nothing.

If you are a sole trader then any income tax will be covered in your personal tax return.

However if you have a limited company then you (as a director) will be responsible for paying your staff's (i.e. you again) National Insurance and Income Tax amounts. Your accountant should be able to calculate the amounts but you (as a director) will have to actually pay it.

VAT Return

If you charge VAT on your services then you will have complete a VAT return.

Each return needs to be made quarterly and actually consists of two parts; (i) the actual return using an on-line HMRC portal and (ii) the associated payment. It is normally due 4 to 5 weeks after the quarter end but the VAT office will send you an email reminder

If you keep good records then you should be able to calculate the figures, make the return and pay the amounts yourself.

Companies House Annual Return

As the name implies, this is an annual return made to Companies House. They do send you a reminder so you do not forgot.

It is only required if you run your own limited company. (If you use an umbrella company then they will complete the return).

It is focused on the internal running and structure of your company and it covers the following items:

- Director details
- Type of company
- Registered address
- Share Capital
- List of shareholders

Approaching the End of a Contract – Should I Stay or Go?

All contracts must come to an end unfortunately.

Therefore as you approach the end of a contract you will need to understand whether the client will renew you or not, as well as whether you actually want to be renewed?

(Although from experience you will probably get some 'vibes' on whether the client will want to renew you during the life of a contract).

However the decision on whether you want to renew is something you will have to make yourself.

The Client Does Not Extend You

There could be a variety of reasons for this. For example the reason you were brought in has gone (e.g. the project has ended or the interim role is not required any more), you have been replaced by an internal permanent member of staff, budgets have been cut or the client does not think you have performed that well.

If you are told you are not being renewed then it will be upsetting and it does hurt but you must be professional. (Remember the importance of protecting your reputation from earlier).

- Therefore do not burn bridges and do your best to leave on good terms. (Again remember the importance of protecting your reputation).

- Work hard to ensure that there is a full handover of your work to whoever is replacing you

- While it sounds counter-intuitive, do not make clients dependent on you because it annoys the client and impacts your reputation.

In parallel to this, you will need to start to look for another role. The hints and tips in the earlier chapter can be followed here.

You Do Not Want to Be Extended

It is not uncommon for contractors to want to leave without renewing.

This could be for a variety of reasons. For example, you do not like working for the client, the assignment did not turn out as hoped, the boss is horrible, found another assignment and so on.

This is always a tricky situation because this could leave your client in an awkward position.

Therefore if you decide that you are not going to stay then give your client as much notice as possible. I would go for a minimum of six weeks prior to your end date. I would also tell them face-to-face and then confirm in email.

The client will no doubt want to know why you are leaving. You should be as open as possible although you will require some level of tact especially if the problem is with the client.

In a similar manner to the above:

- Do not burn bridges and do your best to leave on good terms. (Remember the importance of protecting your reputation).

- Work as hard as you can to ensure that there is a full handover of your work to whoever is replacing you.

- While it sounds counter-intuitive, do not make clients dependent on you because it annoys the client and impacts your reputation.

You Are BeingExtended

If you have been offered an extension and you are happy to be extended then the agency, consultancy or even the end-client will provide you with details of the extension.

Normally it is the same conditions as your current contract but for an extended period of time.

However it is not uncommon for a contractor to request a rate rise. If so then please tread carefully. I would suggest speaking to your manager to explain why you feel you deserve a rise. If the manager says "no" then gracefully accept the decision. Do not try and blackmail the client (e.g. if you do not give me an extra 5% then I will leave) because you could then find yourself leaving very quickly as well as getting a reputation for being hard to work with.

Once everything is agreed then a contract extension agreement will be prepared for all parties to sign.

A Few Other Points to Remember

There are a few other points to remember,

Keep Networking

Always keep networking with fellow contractors, clients, industry groups and on social media. It is important to keep your profile as high as possible.

Maintain Your Cash Buffer

Keep monitoring and (if necessary) topping up your cash buffer to mitigate against any issues such as gaps in employment and invoices being paid late.

Keep Monitoring Your Personal Finances

Keep monitoring your personal finances such as your pensions and your public domain, professional indemnity and employer liability insurances. Also remember that your personal circumstances may have changed as well which could mean you need to review your arrangements.

Keep your CV Up-to-Date

Keep your CV up-to-date so it is immediately ready to be issued if required.

Keep Your Web-Site Up to Date

Ensure your web-site is kept up-to-date.

Keep Your LinkedIn Page Up to Date

Ensure your LinkedIn page is kept up-to-date.

Remember to Look After Yourself

This is often the area forgotten by contractors but there three items I would like to mention.

Keep the Cash Buffer Healthy

I know I keep mentioning this but it is important. It will provide mitigation against gaps between assignments.

Look After Yourself Personally

Remember, it is lonely working for yourself as a contractor. Do not spread yourself thinly, and try and take holidays and/or rest days.

Do Not Be Afraid to Ask for Help and Assistance

There are various social media websites, mentors, and other people who are more than willing to help you.

Key Points

- Maintain your reputation because it will help you get work.
- Keep your skills up-to-date.
- Manage your business affairs on day-to-

---

day basis; viz: invoicing, paying your suppliers, paying yourself and manage your expenses.

- Ensure the regular business events are performed; viz: year-end accounts, paying corporation tax, VAT returns, PAYE/NI returns and the Companies House return.

- Remember all contracts come to an end. The client may decide to either extend you or let you go. You also need to decide whether you want to be extended.

- Keep networking to ensure your profile is high in the industry.

- Keep monitoring and (if necessary) topping up your cash buffer.

- Keep monitoring your personal finances such as your pensions and your public domain, professional indemnity and employer liability insurances.

- Keep your CV up-to-date so it is immediately ready to be issued if required.

- Ensure your web-site is kept up-to-date.

- Ensure your LinkedIn page is kept up-to-date.

- Finally look after yourself. Do not spread yourself thinly, take holidays and do not be afraid to ask for help.

Need Any Advice?

I hope that you enjoyed reading this book and found it interesting?

If you would like any further advice on moving to contracting (or any have feedback on this book) then please email me on

paul.taylor.contracting@gmail.com

What You Need to Consider Before You Go Contracting

Have you thought about going freelance, interim management or contracting but you are nervous about making the jump?

- Is it a good choice for you?

- How to set yourself up as a contractor?

- How to get your first assignment?

- How to operate on a day-to-day basis?

This is where this book comes in. By the end of this book, you will have a good indication of whether contract is the right fit for you and what is required to make the 'jump' from permanent employment into contract work.

About the Author

Paul is a freelance contractor focused on change management with nearly 30 years' experience of which over 11 have been as a contractor.

He has worked on various projects such as operating model design, product design, outsourcing and business change across a variety of businesses such as financial services, oil/gas, charities and professional bodies.

Paul has provided consultancy to start-ups and he is a director for two of these firms.

Paul has chaired a number of industry bodies around management, book judging, start-ups, and entrepreneurship.

Finally Paul has worked for various trade bodies writing course materials. He obtained an MBA from the Open University in 1999.

Printed in Poland
by Amazon Fulfillment
Poland Sp. z o.o., Wrocław

54310067R00060